SOUND THINKING

MUSIC FOR SIGHT-SINGING AND EAR TRAINING

BY PHILIP TACKA AND
MICHEÁL HOULAHAN

BOOSEY & HAWKES

AN IMAGEM COMPANY

DISTRIBUTED BY

HAL•LEONARD®
CORPORATION
7777 W. BLUEMOUND RD. P.O. BOX 13819 MILWAUKEE, WI 53213

Philip Tacka is currently a Visiting Assistant Professor in the Department of Fine Arts at Georgetown University, Washington, D.C. He has earned a D.M.A. from The Catholic University of America and diplomas from the Kodály Pedagogical Institute, Kecskemét, Hungary, and the Kodály Center of America, where he served as Coordinator of Academic Affairs 1986-1987, and Summer Course Director 1985-1987. He has also served on the faculty of Massachusetts Institute of Technology as a Professorial Lecturer in Musicology.

Micheál Houlahan holds a Ph.D. in Music Theory and a Master of Music in Music Education from The Catholic University of America, an honors degree from Dublin, Ireland, and Fellowship and Licentiate Diplomas from Trinity College and London College of Music. He was awarded a Fulbright Scholarship and an Irish Arts Council Scholarship. He earned a diploma from both the Zoltan Kodály Center Pedagogical Institute, Kechemét, Hungary, and the Kodály Center of America where he served on the Summer Faculty in 1987.

Both authors have served independently as consultants to the Educational Office of the John F. Kennedy Center for the Performing Arts, Washington, D.C., the Alexandria, Virginia Public Schools, the Archdiocese of Washington, D.C., the University of Oklahoma, the University of Texas at Austin, and New York University. Both are currently teaching at Georgetown University.

Corrected edition, 1991

ACKNOWLEDGEMENTS

Both volumes of *Sound Thinking: Music for Sight-Singing and Ear Training* were used in undergraduate and graduate courses prior to publication. Many valuable suggestions were received which were incorporated into the final manuscript. Our thanks are due to the teachers, administrators, and institutions who made this field testing possible:

Dean Elaine Walter
Professor Cyrilla Barr
The Benjamin T. Rome School of Music
The Catholic University of America, Washington, D.C.

The Fine Arts Department
Georgetown University, Washington, D.C.

Foundation for Aesthetic Music Education
Kodály Summer Courses at Festival Hill
      in Round Top, Texas

Of the many individuals whe have supported our efforts, we express our gratitude in particular to Alice Trimmer for her editorial guidance and vision; to Crystal Waters for her time and expertise at the computer; and to Miriam Flaherty for her constant advice and support.

To Miriam C. Flaherty

CONTENTS VOLUME 1

CONTENTS VOLUME 2

Introduction

All of the musical examples in *Sound Thinking: Music for Sight-Singing and Ear Training* are drawn from folk songs and art music encompassing a wide range of historical eras. The examples can be used for developing a variety of skills including sight-reading, dictation, musical memory, rhythmic reading, formal analysis, part singing, and improvisation.

The musical material in this collection is arranged in a sequential manner. The examples begin with patterns based on the minor third and progress through pentatonic, diatonic, and modal scales; modulation and chromaticism. The collection is divided into two volumes, each suitable for a semester's study. Volume 1 covers material through the extended pentatonic scale. Volume 2 begins with more complex pentatonic materials and progresses through modal and diatonic music. Rhythmic elements are presented in a similarly structured fashion, beginning with simple groupings of eighth and quarter notes and progressing through compound meter and patterns including sixteenth notes and syncopation. Each rhythmic element is practiced separately before being integrated with melodic elements. New musical elements are not introduced until ample practice has been provided. Because of this careful structuring of musical material, the two volumes of *Music for Sight-Singing and Ear Training* promote greater confidence in the student and provide a more solid basis for skill development than do sight-reading methods that begin with the entire diatonic scale.

Special Features

Each new element is presented in the following way:

1. Characteristic reductions of melodic patterns appear with each chapter opener. These may be practiced separately as preparation for reading them in the context of musical examples. Both melodic and rhythmic patterns were determined as being characteristic of American folk music by an analysis of the pitch and rhythmic content in the 355 folk songs in *Sail Away* and *150 American Folk Songs*, both published by Boosey & Hawkes.

2. Chapter openers also include lists of terms and concepts that might be introduced during the study of that chapter. Not all of the concepts listed will be covered in the musical examples of that chapter; it is expected that many elements will need prior discussion and review for some time before the students will be ready to read them.

Within each chapter many examples appear in more than one key. All staff placements in Volume 1 are in treble clef. Reading the transposed examples helps the student disassociate specific intervals with a particular staff placement and facilitates later reading in various clefs. Once the full diatonic scale is introduced, the teacher should help students determine the *do* placement before reading each example.

Suggestions for Use

This text can be used as a text for college ear training classes, as a supplementary text for high school instrumental and choral groups, or for advanced general music classes in middle school through high school. Because of the carefully structured introduction of new musical concepts, both volumes are suitable for use as self-instruction or review books by adults who wish to improve their music reading skills.

Although the sequence of musical elements introduced in these texts is based on the Kodály concept, the wide range of styles in the examples make them entirely suitable for use with any sight-singing system, including numbers and letter names as well as solfa syllables.

Hand signs can help in orienting students to intervallic relationships through added visual and physical reinforcement.

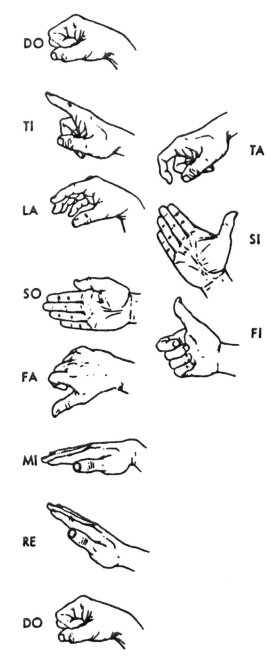

From SIGHT AND SOUND
Arpad Darazs and Stephen Jay
© Copyright 1965 by Boosey & Hawkes, Inc.

Rhythmic examples may be practiced using tapping, enunciating the rhythms on a neutral syllable, or counting by numbers. The examples may also be practiced using rhythm names. A frequently used system of rhythm names is shown below.

Rhythmic element	Rhythm name
♩	ta
♫	ti-ti
𝅗𝅥	ta-a
𝅝	ta-a-a-a
♬♬	ti-ri-ti-ri
♩♬	ti-ti-ri
♬♩	ti-ri-ti
♫	tim-ri
♫.	ri-tim
♪ ♩ ♪	ti-ta-ti (syn-co-pah)
♩. ♪	tie-ti
♪ ♩.	ti-tie
³♫♩	tri-o-la

Rhythm names for compound meter

♫♩	ti-ti-ti
♩ ♪	ta-ti
♪. ♪ ♪	tim-ri-ti

Mastery of ear training and sight-singing normally takes many hours of practice. Practice sessions can be made more efficient by using a variety of practice techniques. Suggestions for the student on practicing rhythmic and melodic elements are given in the "How to Practice" sections below. Classroom strategies for developing techniques in musical memory, dictation and sight-singing may be found on pages 7 through 14. Many of these strategies can be used in individual practice by the students as well. Practicing in small groups is invaluable for students. In addition to sharpening their listening skills by evaluating each other's performances, students who practice for their peers will find that they are far more secure when called on in class.

For more comprehensive teaching suggestions related to preparation, presentation, and practice for each of the elements introduced in these volumes, see Tacka and Houlahan's: *Sound Thinking: Musical Skill Development Through the Kodály Concept* (Boosey & Hawkes, © 1995).

How to Practice Melodic Elements

1. Sing with syllables. Conduct while singing to keep a steady beat.

2. Sing with syllables, using hand signs.

3. Sing with rhythm names, using hand signs.

4. Sing a pattern or show it with hand signs. Ask another person to sing it back.

5. Memorize an entire exercise and notate it without referring to the book. First analyze the form by looking for repeated and similar parts. This will simplify the task.

6. Select a phrase of music from the book. One person plays the selection, deliberately making a melodic mistake. Another person follows the score and locates the error.

How to Practice Rhythmic Elements

1. Speak the rhythm patterns while tapping the beat.

2. Speak the rhythm while conducting.

3. Echo patterns clapped by someone else.

4. Identify the meter and rhythm patterns clapped or sung by another person.

5. Change the rhythm pattern from one into another. One person writes a 16 beat pattern then claps a slightly different pattern. The other person must identify where the changes occur.

6. Improvise rhythm patterns. First select a meter and length for the pattern, then decide what rhythmic form (for example, ABA or ABAB) to use.

7. Write out the rhythm of one of the selections from the book. Study the form to identify repeated patterns. Memorize it and write it out from memory.

8. Perform a rhythmic canon. Practice the canon in the following way:

    a. Say the rhythm names while clapping the rhythm.
    b. Think the rhythm names and clap the rhythm.
    c. Think and clap the rhythm in canon while another person claps the second part of the canon.
    d. Clap the rhythm in canon with someone else.
    e. Perform the rhythmic canon by yourself. Tap one part with one hand and use a pencil to tap the other part with the other hand.

The Development of Musical Memory

Musical memory plays an important role in accurate singing and in the ability to recall a pattern for the purposes of dictation. The following techniques can be helpful.

1. Memorizing by hand signs
2. Memorizing from rhythmic and staff notation
3. Memorizing by ear

Memorizing by Hand Signs

1. Show typical melodic patterns and ask the students to sing patterns back. Start with short patterns such as s - l - s - m or m - f - m - r - m.
2. When the melodic patterns are mastered, progress to four-bar and eight-bar melodies.
3. Show a melody in hand signs. Select pentatonic melodies or rounds. The students sing the melody in canon using solfa or absolute letter names and write down the example from memory.
4. The teacher may also give the starting pitch of a key and ask the students to sing a melody with absolute letter names while using hand signs.

Memorizing from Staff Notation

1. The students look at a score and memorize a short fragment of a musical example, using hand signs.
2. The teacher sings the unknown part of the example. Students sing the memorized motifs.
3. Students then write the melody down on staff paper. At a more advanced level, the students can write the example in another key using a different clef.
4. Look at an example using familiar elements. Memorize the example without singing or playing.

Memorizing by Ear

Memorizing by ear is more difficult than memorizing from notation as it involves no visual aid. Melodies used for memorizing by ear should be easier than those used with notation. Extracts should be played on the piano or another instrument and sung a few times. The following procedures may be used for both rhythmic and melodic memorization.

1. Students identify the meter.

2. Students identify the ending and starting pitches.

3. Students sing the example and conduct.

4. Students sing the example with hand signs.

5. Students sing the example with absolute pitch names and hand signs.

6. Students sing the example with rhythm names.

7. Students write the exercise or play it back on the piano. Later, the example may be transposed.

The teacher may also play a melody and ask the students to sing it back in canon at the unison while memorizing the example. Later canons at other intervals may be used.

When students have gained experience in unison memory work, they can begin to memorize two-part extracts. Accompaniments may be drawn from a rhythmic pattern, a rhythmic or melodic ostinato, chord roots, a contrapuntal melodic line, or typical cadential idioms in modal or harmonic music. Memory work should also include three and four-part work.

Procedures:

1. Sing the selected extracts in two parts.

2. Memorize one part silently using solfa.

3. Sing the part out loud while conducting.

4. Practice the other part following steps 1 through 3.

5. Sing both parts in a group and then as solos, using both solfa and note names.

6. Write down both parts of the extract.

7. Sing one part and play the other on the piano, or sing one part and show the second part with hand signs.

Sight-Singing

Before each exercise the teacher should practice basic rhythmic and melodic patterns from the sight-reading exercise with the students while the students follow the staff notation. Difficult rhythms should be practiced with a suitable rhythmic ostinato or subdivision of the beat. Sing these preparatory exercises in the same key as the reading example. Exercises may be sung in solfège, letter names and neutral syllables. The following procedure may be used for sight-reading new material.

1. Make the students aware of the meter and key. Choose an appropriate tempo.

2. Discuss the form of the exercise. Look for repeated patterns.

3. Students think through the entire melody.

4. Students conduct or use hand signs while thinking through the melody.

5. Students sing the exercise while conducting.

The sight-singing exercise may be memorized and notated. Students should continually practice reading melodic patterns with or without a specific rhythm. Teachers should devise a variety of ways to practice a reading exercise. For example: reading the melody backwards; reading a unison melody while clapping a rhythmic ostinato; singing a melody in canon at the fifth with only the first voice given.

Dictation

Dictation is closely linked to the development of musical memory, inner hearing, and reading and writing skills. It is important to spend time developing the student's memory as this skill is essential for dictation. Initial dictations should be based on patterns that have been memorized by the students. As the student's memory develops the teacher can begin more formal dictation practice. At first the melody should be sung by the students before notating it, so that the teacher may be sure the students are hearing it accurately.

The following procedures may be used for melodic dictation.

1. The teacher prepares the key of the dictation with hand signs and staff notation.

2. The teacher shows typical melodic patterns extracted from the melody used for dictation, and the students sing in solfa and letter names. At the beginning stages of formal dictation the teacher may also give the student a score with the barlines indicated and certain notes or rhythms filled in.

3. The teacher plays the melody on the piano or another instrument.

4. Students determine the final note and the beginning note as well as some or all of the following, as appropriate: mode, melodic cadences, melodic contour, patterns, and meter.

5. Students sing the melody using solfa and absolute letter names.

6. Students sing the melody with rhythm names and hand signs.

7. Students sing the melody from memory.

8. Students write the melody down.

9. Students sing the melody from their score. This melody may be used to practice other skills such as transposing or practicing the intervals in the melody.

   In addition to notating the rhythms of melodies accurately, students should also practice rhythmic dictation separately from melodic dictation. The following procedures may be used.

1. The teacher plays a melody on the piano while students establish the meter and the number of bars.

2. The teacher plays and the students conduct.

3. Students conduct and sing using rhythm syllables.

4. Students write the rhythm.

5. The teacher plays once more while the students follow the score.

Part Singing

Those who always sing in unison never learn to sing in correct pitch. Correct unison singing can, paradoxically, be learned only by singing in two parts.

    - Zoltan Kodály (Foreward of *Let Us Sing Correctly*)

Singing and playing part music are important aspects of musical training. These skills enable the student to learn to hear several voices simultaneously.

The following procedures may be used for developing two-part singing.

1. Sing folk songs or other exercises while clapping the beat or the rhythm.

2. Sing folk songs, dividing the singing by phrases in call-and-response style. This enables Group A to hear what Group B sings, and vice versa.

3. Add a rhythmic or melodic ostinato to folk songs. This can be done in five stages.

   a. Students sing the melody while the teacher claps the ostinato.

   b. Students and the teacher exchange parts.

   c. Divide the students into two groups; one group sings and another performs the ostinato.

   d. Two students perform the song and ostinato.

   e. One student sings one voice and claps the rhythmic ostinato or plays the melodic ostinato on the piano.

4. Students clap a series of rhythmic patterns while singing a known song.

5. Sing in two parts from hand signs. This helps students see the intervals spatially.

6. Sing simple pentatonic folk songs in canon.

7. Sing a well-known song and at the same time clap various rhythms that the teacher points to. The students may also read an exercise while the teacher improvises an extended rhythmic ostinato. The students must sing and listen at the same time, then try to recall the rhythmic pattern. Start with simple, familiar patterns.

8. Sing one part and clap the second part simultaneously.

9. Two-part singing:

   a. If the two-part selection is a folk song, teach the song first either by rote or from the music, then teach the second part.

   b. Divide the class into two groups. Group A sings the top line while Group B sings the bottom. Reverse.

   c. Group A sing the bottom line and Group B claps the top. Reverse

   d. Perform the work as a group and then with soloists. Individuals may then sing any part while clapping the other part or may sing one part and play the second part on the piano.

PITCH

More Complex Pentatonic Melodies

Melodic Patterns

d' - l - s - m - r - d - $l,$ - $s,$ d' - l - s - m - r - d - $s,$

$s,$ - $l,$ - d - r - m - s - l - d' $s,$ - d - r - m - s - l - d'

d' - s s - d'

d' - m m - d'

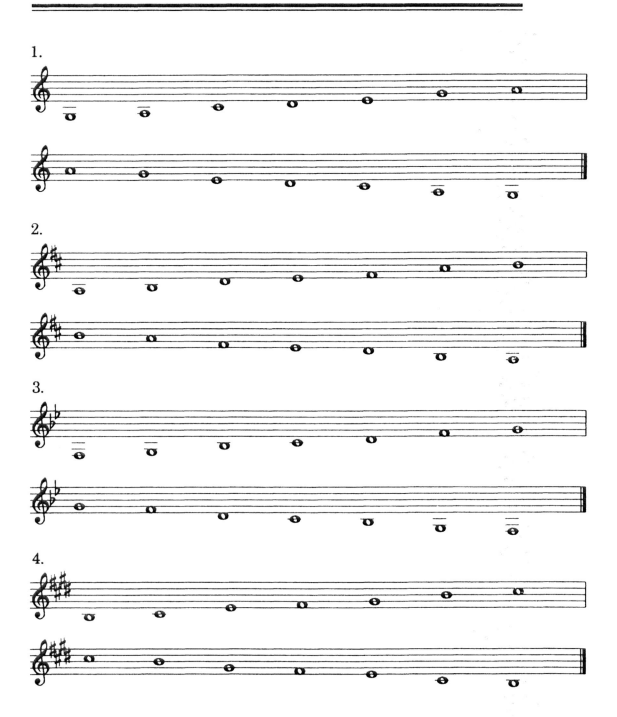

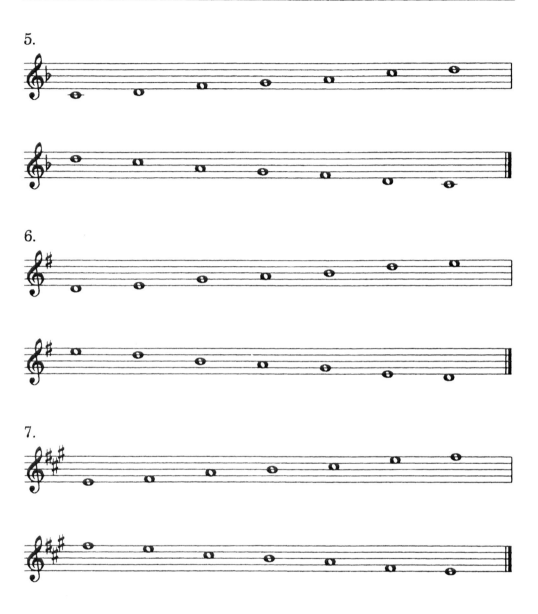

14.

15.

25.

26.

PITCH

Stick Notation

do' - so - fa - mi - re - do - la, - so, (*do* pentachord)

do' - la - so - fa - mi - re - do - la, - so, (*do* hexachord)

Selected Melodic Patterns

l - s - f - m - r - d	*d - f*
d - r - m - f - s	*f - d*
f - r	*l - f*
r - f	*f - l*

Terms and Concepts

fa
half step or semi-tone
pentachord
hexachord
flat sign

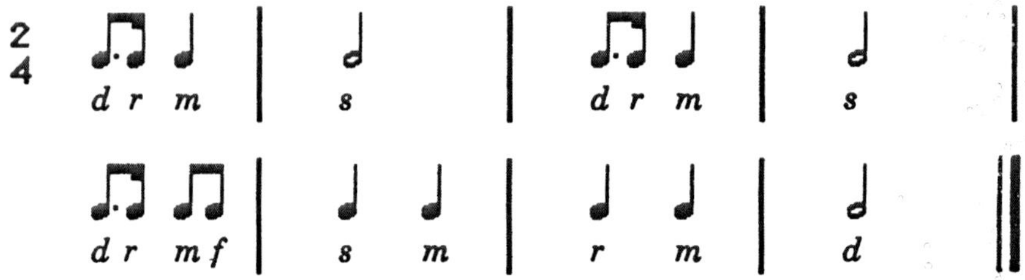

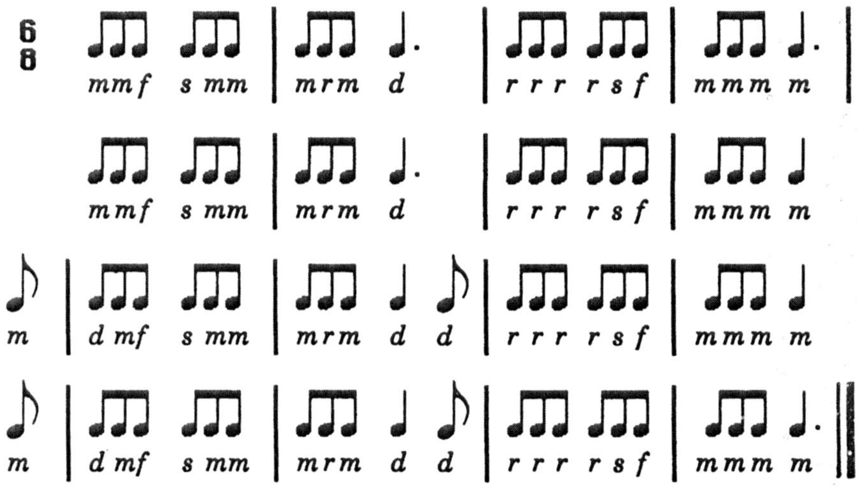

3. $\frac{4}{4}$

d r | m m m m r | m m r d

d | r r r d | m s ‿

s | l l s s f | m m r d

s | m m m r | r d ‿ ‖

4. $\frac{2}{4}$

s m l s s | m s d | r m f r r | m s s s s |

m s s s s | f l l l l | m s s m m | r d d ‖

5. 4/4

m m f s | s f m r |

d d r m | m r r |

m m f s | s f m r |

d d r m | r d d |

r r m d | r m f m d |

r m f m r | d r s, |

m m f s | s f m r |

d d r m | r d d ‖

PITCH

Staff Notation

do' - so - fa - mi - re - do - la, - so, (*do* pentachord)

do' - la - so - fa - mi - re - do - la, - so, (*do* hexachord)

1.

2.

3.

4.

5.   Beethoven

15.

16.

17.

18.

19.

20.

21.

22.

23.

24.

25.

26.

27.

28.

40.

PITCH

Stick Notation
Diatonic Scale

do' - ti - la - so - fa - mi - re - do - ti, - la, - so,

Selected Melodic Patterns

s, - l, - t, - d   *s, - t, - d*
d - t, - l,   *r - t, - s,*
r - t, - d - l,   *s, - t, - r*
d - t, - r   *m - t,*

Terms and Concepts
ti
whole step
half step
passing notes
auxiliary notes
all absolute letter names
enharmonic note names
la pentachord
la hexachord
scale
major scale
minor scale
key signature
major key signatures
circle of fifths
transposition

1. 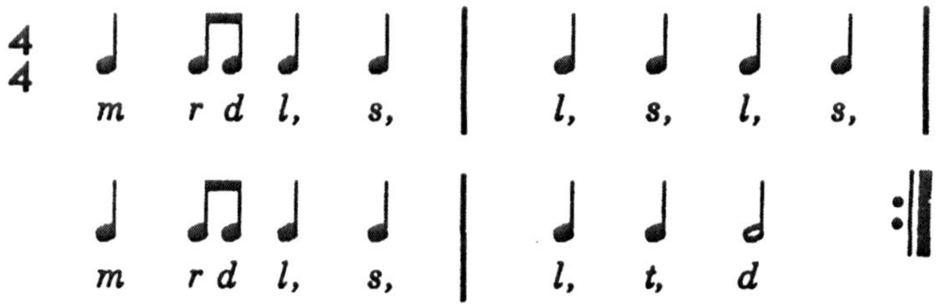
4
4
m r d l, s, l, s, l, s,
m r d l, s, l, t, d

2. 
2
4
mm mm r dd t, l,
mm s m r dd t, l,
t, d r dd t, l,
t, d r dd t, l,

3. $\frac{2}{4}$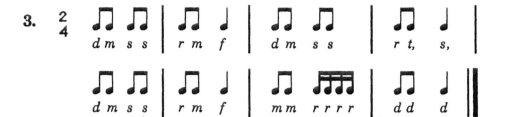

4. $\frac{3}{4}$

5.

4
4
s, | d d r t, | d d |
m m f r	m d r
m m r r	d d t, t,
l, l, t, t,	d d
m m f r	m d
m m f r	m d r
m m r r	d d t, t,
l, l, t, t,	d	

PITCH

Staff Notation
Diatonic Scale

do' - ti - la - so - fa - mi - re - do - ti, - la, - so,

3.

4.

5.

6.

9.

10.

11.

PITCH

re Pentatonic Scale

re - mi - so - la - do' - re' - (mi')

Terms and Concepts

re pentatonic scale

1.

2. Dorian Mode Example

3.

4.

5.

PITCH

Dorian Mode

re - mi - fa - so - la - ti - do' - re'

comparative scale

la, - ti, - do - re - mi - fi - so - la

Terms and Concepts

dorian mode

1.

2.

3.

6.

PITCH

so Pentatonic Scale

so, - la, - do - re - mi - so

Terms and Concepts

so pentatonic scale

7.

PITCH

Mixolydian Mode

so, - la, - ti, - do - re - mi - fa - so - la

comparative scale

do - re - mi - fa - so - la - ta - do

Terms and Concepts

mixolydian scale

1.

2.

3.

4.

5.

6.

PITCH

la Pentatonic Scale

la, - do - re - mi - so - la

Terms and Concepts

la pentatonic scale

6.

PITCH

Aeolian Mode

la, - ti , - do - re - mi - fa - so - la

Natural Minor Scale

6.

7.

PITCH

The Natural Minor Scale

la, - ti ,- do - re - mi - fa - so - la

The Harmonic Minor Scale

la, - ti, - do - re - mi - fa - si - la

The Melodic Minor Scale

la, - ti, - do - re - mi - fi - si - la - so - fa - mi - re - do - ti, - la,

Terms and Concepts

natural minor scale
harmonic minor scale
melodic minor scale
minor key signatures
relative keys
parallel keys
accidentals
natural sign

$\frac{6}{8}$ meter

compound duple, triple, and quadruple meter
triplets
double sharp
double flat

4.   Purcell

6. O Bone Jesu   Palestrina

7.   Haydn

PITCH

Musical Examples
Using Altered Tones

do - di - re - ri - mi - fa - fi - so - si - la - ta - ti - do

do - ra - re - ma - mi - fa - so - law - la - ta - ti - do

Terms and Concepts

altered tones
bass clef
numerical identification of intervals
quality identification of intervals
inversion of intervals
consonance
dissonance

1. Solvieg's Song   Grieg

2.   Brahms

3.   Piano Sonata, Op. 109,II   Beethoven

4.   Canon, String Quartet Op. 76 No.2, III   Haydn

5. Contradance K. 267

Mozart

6. Mass in E♭

Schubert

7. Farewell Symphony   Haydn

8. Frühlingstraum, Op. 89, No. 11   Schubert

9.   Der Blumenstrauss, Op. 47, No. 5   Mendelssohn

10.   Beethoven

11.

Purcell

12. Caldara

13. Quintet, K. 406 Mozart

14. Du Ring am mein Finger, Op. 42, No. 4 Schumann

Cranford 17th Century

16.

Morley

HARMONY

Musical Examples Using
Tonic and Dominant Triads

Terms and Concepts

tonic function
dominant function

Accompany these examples with tonic and dominant notes.

1. Jim Along Josie

2. Derry Ding Dong Dason (Canon)

3. Christmas Greeting

4. God Bless All

5. Skip to My Lou

6. I's the B'y

7. Love Somebody

8. I's the B'y (minor)

9. Love Somebody (minor)

10. Down in the Valley

11. Skating Away

12. Marmotte   Beethoven

Sing the top part in your own range.
Play the bottom part on the piano.

13. Rondo

Mozart

HARMONY

Musical Examples Using Tonic, Dominant, and Subdominant Triads

Terms and Concepts

subdominant function

Accompany these examples with tonic, subdominant, and dominant notes.

1.

2.

3.

4. Music Alone Shall Live

5. The Zebra Dun

Sing and analyze.

6.

7.

8.

Mozart

ROUNDS AND CANONS

Terms and Concepts

4.

5.

6.

7.

8.

9.

13. Traditional

14.

17.

18.

MODULATING MELODIES

Musical Examples
that Modulate
to Closely Related Keys

4.

5.

6.

7. Haydn

8.   P. Hayes

9. Marienwürmchen, Op. 79 No. 14 — Schumann

10. Divertimento, K. 131 — Mozart

11. Quartet No. 2, Op. 18 No. 2   Beethoven

12. Wachet Auf

J. S. Bach

EARLY MUSIC

Musical Examples
in Renaissance Style
to Sing and Play

1. Bransle

2. Canon   Tallis

3. Hungarian Dance

(accompaniment)

130

4. Troubadour Song "Quant il rossignols" 13th Century

Quant il ros - si - gnols s'es cri - e
Qui nos des - duit de - - son chant.
Join - tes main - mer ci - li cri - e,
Car on - ques rien n'a - - mai - tant.

5. Ut queant laxix

Ut que - ant la - xix Re - so - na - re fib - ris,
Mi - - ra ge sto - rum Fa - mu - li tu - o - rum
Sol - - ve pol - lu - ti La - bi - i - re - a - tum,
San - cte Jo - an - nes.

6. Non nobis Domine   Wm. Byrd

Non   no - bis   Do - mi-ne,   non   no - bis

sed no-mi-ni   tu - o   da   glo - ri - am

sed no-mi-ni   tu - o   da   glo - ri - am.

7. Orientibus partibus   (1250)

O - ri - en - tis   par - ti - bus.

ad - ven - ta - vit   a - si - nus,

pul - cher   et   for - tis - si - mus,

sar - ci - nis   ap - tis - si - mus

Hez,   sir   as - ne,   hez!

"Ce fut en May" Trouvere Song

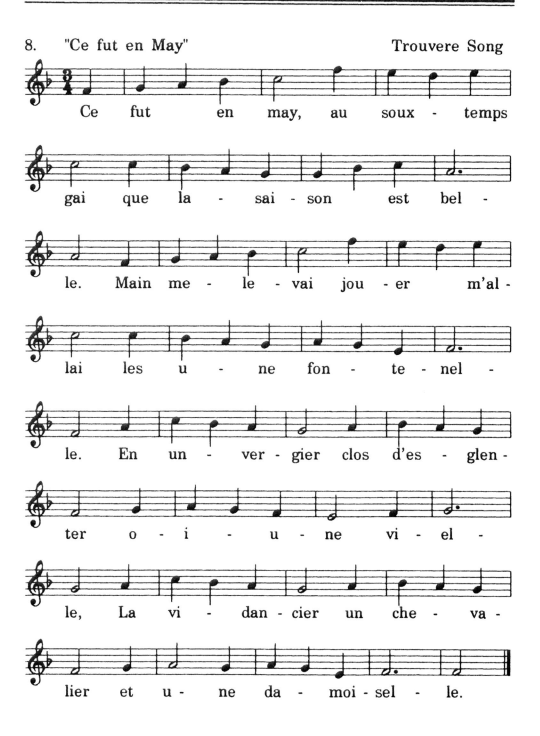

Ce fut en may, au soux - temps
gai que la - sai - son est bel -
le. Main me - le - vai jou - er m'al -
lai les u - ne fon - te - nel -
le. En un - ver - gier clos d'es - glen -
ter o - i - u - ne vi - el -
le, La vi - dan - cier un che - va -
lier et u - ne da - moi - sel - le.

9. "Ave Maris Stella" Gregorian Hymn

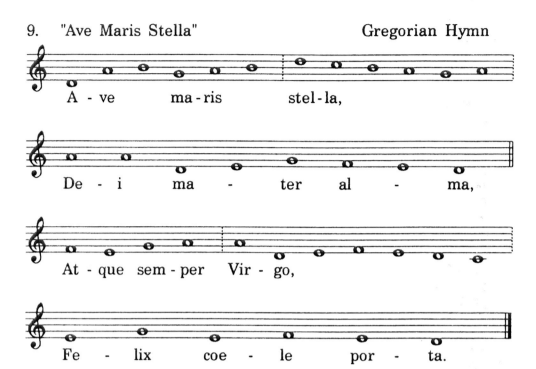

A - ve ma - ris stel - la,

De - i ma - ter al - ma,

At - que sem - per Vir - go,

Fe - lix coe - le por - ta.

10. "Pange Lingua"

Pan - ge lin - gua glo - ri - o - si

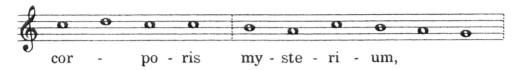

cor - po - ris my - ste - ri - um,

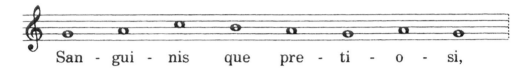

San - gui - nis que pre - ti - o - si,

quem in mun - di pre - ti - um

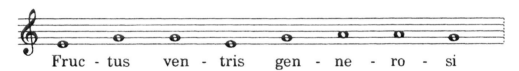

Fruc - tus ven - tris gen - ne - ro - si

Rex ef - fu - dit gen - ti - um.

11. L'homme arme

12. Sellinger's Round

Anonymous

13. In Dulci Jubilo

Chorale Tune

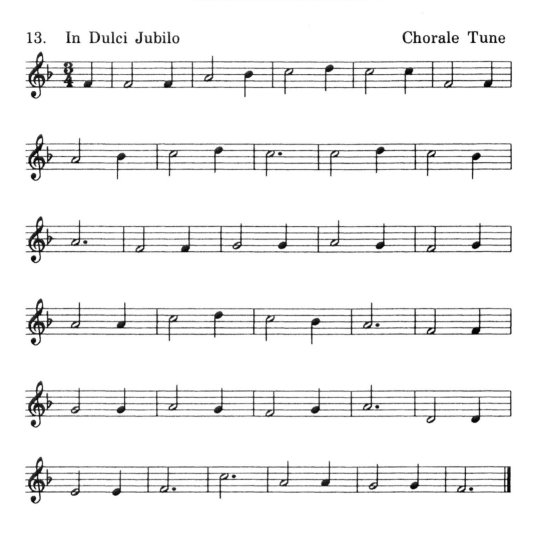

14. Omnis Mundus   from Piae Cantiones (1582)

15. Personant Hodie   Piae Cantiones

16. Robin Adam de la Halle

17. Robin Adam de la Halle

18. Sumer Is Icumen In

19. Greensleeves   Anonymous

20.

Il - lu - mi -na o - culos me - - - os, ne

un-quam ob-dor-mi - am in mor - - - te.

Begin the canon in measure two a major second below the starting pitch.

21. Canon   Josquin de Pres

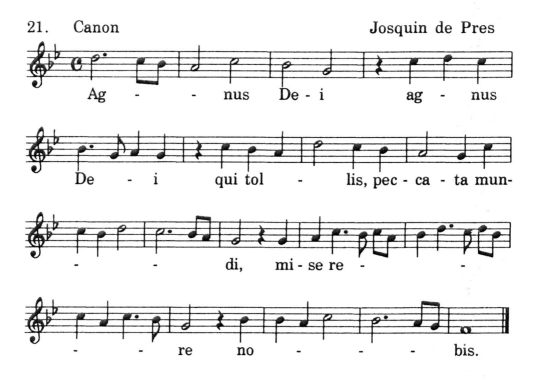

Ag - - nus De - i   ag - nus

De - i   qui tol - lis, pec - ca - ta mun-

- - di,   mi - se re - -

- - re   no - - - bis.

CLASSICAL REPERTOIRE

Selected Musical Examples
that May Be Sung
and Incorporated into
Listening Lessons

1. New World Symphony, II   Dvorák

2. Peer Gynt Suite, "Morning"   Grieg

3. Pictures at an Exhibition, "Promenade"   Moussorgsky

4. Pictures at an Exhibition, "Great Gate of Kiev"   Moussorgsky

5. The Crane
Tchaikovsky

6. Symphony No. 4
Tchaikovsky

7. Eine Kleine Nachtmusik, IV
Mozart

9. Finlandia   Sibelius

10. Where'er You Walk, Semele   Handel

11. Petrouchka   Stravinsky

1.   2.

12.

1.   2.

13. Dance of the Furies

Gluck

14. Hungarian Dance V

Brahms

15. Symphony No. 94, "Surprise"

Haydn

16 March from Aida   Verdi

17. Symphony No. 8, "Unfinished"   Schubert

18. Little Fugue in G minor   J. S. Bach

19. Cello Concerto in D — Haydn

20. The Trout — Schubert

21. — Brahms

22. Symphony No.7
Beethoven

23. Symphony No. 40
Mozart

24. Brandenburg Concerto
J. S. Bach

Haydn

26. St. Anthony's Chorale   Haydn

fine

D.C.